IMAGES

of America

BIG TIMBER

IMAGES
of America

BIG TIMBER

Leslie Paulson Stryker and
the Crazy Mountain Museum

ARCADIA
PUBLISHING

Published by Arcadia Publishing
Charleston, South Carolina

Library of Congress Control Number: 2008935196

For all general information contact Arcadia Publishing at:
Telephone 843-853-2070
Fax 843-853-0044
E-mail sales@arcadiapublishing.com
For customer service and orders:
Toll-Free 1-888-313-2665

Visit us on the Internet at www.arcadiapublishing.com

To my darling girls, Katherine and Elizabeth. I shall love you forever; you are and always will be the absolute pride and joys of my life!

CONTENTS

Acknowledgments   6

Introduction   7

1.   Humble Origins   9

2.   Progress and Prosperity   21

3.   Tragedy Strikes   53

4.   Home Sweet Home   59

5.   A Bow, a Fiddle, and a Do-si-do   81

6.   The More It Changes, the More It Stays the Same   105

ACKNOWLEDGMENTS

Books are seldom written alone, and this was no exception. I would like to express thanks and gratitude to the Crazy Mountain Museum for the use of their images and to the many volunteers whose dedication is evident the moment one arrives at the museum. I am so indebted to the curator of the museum, Rita Esp. Rita was so generous with her time; she was invaluable to me from start to finish. Rita, like the many photographs and collectables she lovingly catalogs and exhibits, is priceless. She was a joy to meet and spend time with, and I hope we will always remain friends. The board members of the Crazy Mountain Museum were wonderful in their interest and willingness to allow me to use the museum's research and photographic archives. Unless otherwise noted, all photographs used here are courtesy of the Crazy Mountain Museum Archives.

I actually had two editors at Arcadia: Hannah Carney, who was so encouraging and patient at getting me started (I wish her the best with her new career), and John Poultney, who has been just great. He was a good sport when I ran into photograph scanning problems, and he was wonderfully pushy, encouraging, and patient all at the right moments. Thanks so much to you, John, and the rest of the Arcadia staff who helped get this book published.

Thanks to the people of Big Timber for your continued support of the Crazy Mountain Museum. Your generosity with photographs, memorabilia, and donations keeps this museum a true gem. Many heartfelt thanks to Tim Thigpen, my photographic wizard, for his knowledge, his patience, and his time. Also, to Doug Lair, my thanks for his invaluable insight into the "woolies."

To Michael, my "lost love," many thanks for taking care of Painted Sky and our "paints" while I was busy writing. I could not have done this without all your hard work. To David, my friend and my ex, thanks for all those years you encouraged me to put my thoughts to paper! My love and thanks to Michael B., my "second" brother, for being a wonderful addition to our family and for making our Bob so happy! And to those of you, my newest friends in my new home, who shared this journey with me, thank you so much for your kindness and your interest.

Finally, to my dearest and irreplaceable parents, Roy and Jane; my fantastically adorable brother, Bob; and my sweet and unforgettable grandmother, Frances: there just aren't enough words to express my love for all of you or to thank you all for your love, your encouragement, and your support; you never give up on me. You all and the girls shall remain forever my "True North."

INTRODUCTION

Like the rivers and creeks that surround it ebb and flow, so too has the history of Big Timber, Montana.

Beginning in 1806 when William Clark, of the Lewis and Clark Expedition, first stopped here and named the area Rivers Across because of the merging of the Boulder River and the Big Timber Creek into the Yellowstone River, the town and surrounding area have seen many changes. And yet even today, visitors and residents alike will tell you that Big Timber remains in many ways a place where time stands still.

Those who drive down the main street of town, called McLeod Street after W. F. McLeod, the first permanent homesteader in the Boulder Valley, who arrived in 1882, can see and feel that much has transpired here through the years.

In the beginning, the main inhabitants of the area were the Crow Indians. The Blackfoot and Sioux Indians also traveled in and out of the area. Then slowly, the white man started to arrive. They came in small numbers at first, by wagon trains, stagecoach, and ox team or on horseback. Some of them herded cattle or sheep long distances in order to have a way to make a living and survive, while others chose to bring family heirlooms as a way to keep those they left behind close at heart. It was a difficult journey at best, and there was not much here once they finally arrived.

Originally, the town of Big Timber was a settlement named Dornix by an Irish immigrant. The word Dornix is derived from a Gaelic word, "Durnog," which means "a rock that fits in the hand and is handy for throwing," and even to this day, the ground is littered with just such rocks.

When the Northern Pacific Railroad arrived in 1882, the settlement was relocated (to the present location) and given the name Big Timber. With the completion of the railroad in 1883, the settlement became a town that quickly started to progress and prosper. Not only did the physical size of the town grow, but the population of both people and sheep exploded as well. By 1892, Big Timber was one of the largest exporters of wool in the world. More than 2 million pounds were shipped out by rail that year alone.

By 1894, other commerce was booming as well. The *Big Timber Pioneer* newspaper was started in 1889 and is still in print today. By 1893, the population had doubled to 500. And by 1898, the Sweet Grass County Courthouse had been built and the town could boast of having more varied and numerous businesses than just the essential establishments most new frontier towns had.

Around this time, several of the founding fathers were actively helping mold and shape the town. By using their imaginations and finances to build such things as a wool warehouse, a toll bridge over the Yellowstone River, and several businesses in town, they were helping set the tone for other investors coming into town. It is interesting to note that even the roads in town were paved. Not in the modern-day style with asphalt but with large smooth rocks. It was a very ingenious way to keep the mud roads from washing out. Big Timber was established, prosperous, and continuing to grow.

Then, in 1908, on a windy Big Timber day, tragedy struck the entire town. It should be duly noted that Big Timber and the surrounding areas are typically very windy from late fall until early summer. The area sits between the mountains that create these winds and funnel them along through the area. This particular tragedy happened on Friday, March 13, 1908; it was a massive fire. The fire was started by embers blowing from the smokestack of a train making a stop at the train station. Because of the strong and gusty wind, the embers quickly scattered and set fire to a large rubbish pile near the tracks, which in turn started a grass fire. By then, the winds were spreading embers and starting fires across the entire town. With so many fires all burning at once and in so many different locations, the fire department just could not keep up, and by the time it was finally out (even with the help of some neighboring firemen and their trucks from Livingston), more than one-third of the town was destroyed. It was a devastating blow to everyone but especially to those who lost everything.

Even before the smoke had cleared, the mood of the town was one of survival and determination. Those who had survived without a loss would do all they could to help those who had lost it all. The businessmen of the community started right away to rebuild the businesses that were lost with both financial and physical help. The Northern Pacific Railroad admitted negligence and offered funds to those who had suffered. But even with determination and money, it still took a long time for things to be rebuilt. Many establishments just rebuilt while others took the opportunity to enlarge or improve their businesses and homes. With the vast numbers of buildings and homes involved, it truly took the entire community to pull together to help each other through this tragedy. While the town recovered and changed from the fire, the surrounding areas would also start to see some changes in the ways a living was made.

As the community continued to recover, improve, and change, many new interests would begin. Mining came to the area off and on in the following years. The dreams of striking it rich took men up the Boulder and into the Crazy Mountains. Those seeking riches would come and go in town just like the veins of ore they so desperately searched for. Mining was also responsible for the first murder in the area, which to this day has never been solved.

Also, around this same time, the era of the large sheep ranches was slowly fading. As ranchers lost the rights to lease many of their vast and necessary grazing pastures, the days of the huge bands of sheep slowly came to an end. For many ranchers, the cattle industry seemed a logical alternative. Cattle ranching also meant an increase in the horse business, as horses were commonly used with cattle ranching. Where there are cattle, there are cowboys. And where there are cowboys, the rodeo is not far behind. Big Timber had a local famous rodeo producer who helped get the rodeo started, and the rodeo still remains an annual summer event held at the fairgrounds.

As time moved on, Big Timber became a family-oriented community with many residents coming here from other places. There was an especially large influx of Norwegians, who brought with them a new culture and new ideas for the town. Life in town and on the ranches in the area settled into a mixture of everyday routines scattered with the occasional special event.

Today Big Timber is home to year-round residents as well as summer ones. There are also many ranches both small and large in the area. Residents and visitors alike enjoy all the outdoor activities the area has to offer. The Crazy Mountains and the Boulder Valley play a major role in providing a beautifully scenic playground for many of these activities. Hollywood found the glorious "big screen" scenery in the area and has come to town several times to make movies and a television series. We have several movie stars of our own who live in the area on ranches. There also continue to be generations of the original founding families who live in town or on ranches close by.

Today Big Timber continues to be a wonderful place to live and visit. As people walk through town, they can still see some of the history that helped make it the charming and picturesque place it remains. Regardless of the season, one will find the scenery breathtaking, the town inviting, and the locals warm and friendly. There is no end to the activities one can enjoy under the blue Montana sky.

One

HUMBLE ORIGINS

This is Big Timber, Montana, in 1886 looking south down what would become McLeod Street. The Northern Pacific Railroad came through town and was completed in 1883. The first large building on the left is the Big Timber Hotel, which faces the train depot on what was called Front Street.

The Crow Indians were some of the first inhabitants of the area around Big Timber. This is Chief Plenty Coup, a Crow Indian. As a young man around 1858, Plenty Coup left his village for a two-day walk to the Crazy Mountains. He was on a "vision quest" to ask guidance from the Great Spirit. He went without food and water for four days, and when he finally arrived at the top of Crazy Peak, he received his famous vision. He foresaw that in his lifetime, the buffalo would go away forever, the white man would take and hold his country, and that their cattle would cover the plains. The survival of the Crow people would depend on them siding with the white men and never making war upon them.

This 1871 photograph was taken by W. H. Jackson of the Hayden Party of Fort Parker. The fort, located on Mission Creek, was used as Crow Indian Reservation Headquarters from 1868 until 1875. The Crow Agency was established by the government to house goods and provide services for the Crow Indians. Along with the warehouse were quarters that housed a physician, a carpenter, a farmer, a miller, a blacksmith, and an engineer. There was also a mission building used as a school. In 1825, when the Friendship Treaty was signed, there were an estimated 2,500 Crow Indians in the area; by 1880, all those left in the area would be confined to reservations.

The rugged landscape of the Crazy Mountains adds to the many legends of why they are called the "Crazies." According to one, a white woman went insane after losing her husband and child in a Native American raid. She went up into the mountains and remained there alone for the rest of her days. Another legend tells of the Native Americans calling them the "Mad" Mountains because of their steepness, rugged beauty, and haunting winds. The last theory, based on science, has to do with the geological aspects of the mountain range. Apparently, the rock formations are of a very "old" type and yet the mountains are by geological standards very young. Therefore, it makes no scientific sense, so it is "crazy."

The Yellowstone River near Big Timber is pictured in the 1800s. This beautiful and often fearsome river must have looked much the same to William Clark of the Lewis and Clark Expedition when he and his men traveled in the Big Timber area in mid-July 1806. They were some of the first white men in the area and stopped near Big Timber where the Yellowstone meets the Boulder River. He even named the location where they camped, calling it Rivers Across. While in the area, Clark and his men observed and took notes on the wildlife and cataloged samples of native plants and grasses to take with them back east.

This image of the Yellowstone with the Crazy Mountains in the background shows the massive ice that builds up on the river each winter. While beautiful, it must have proved quite a challenge to cross in the early 1800s. Even in the late 1800s, when a rope ferry was available, it could still be a treacherous event.

The Crazy Mountains are shown with their snowy peaks. The pioneers arrived with dreams, hopes, and wishes for new and prosperous lives in this vast frontier. They traveled over plains and mountains to get here. Some spent their entire life savings to make the trip and start a new life. Most traveled a long way, and once they finally arrived, there was not much to greet them except breathtaking views like these.

NATURAL BRIDGE RANCH IN BOULDER VALLEY NEAR BIG TIMBER MONT. – ROAY PHOTO–

The fertile Boulder Valley area is located south of town. By 1895, settlers were arriving in the area by stagecoach, ox team, horseback, covered wagon, and even on foot. Many herded livestock like sheep or cattle with them on their long and arduous journey. Once they arrived, they faced the even more daunting task of survival under extreme conditions, like harsh winters, the threat of unfriendly Native Americans, primitive living conditions, summer droughts, no medical help, and a lack of available goods and supplies.

A couple sitting on the front stoop of their "new" frontier ranch home are wearing white, usually reserved for special occasions. Perhaps they are newly married and just beginning housekeeping together. Notice the array of building materials used to construct the home. When building a home, most early settlers used whatever was close by or left over after building the barn to construct their home. This home would have been considered fancy because it had a window.

14

Note the curtains on the door of this early log home. Even with all of the harsh conditions and sacrifices this pioneer woman has to deal with every day, she still maintains pride and beauty in her home. Also note the lack of trees in the area. It is possible they were all used to build this home and outbuilding to the right.

This stone house would have been constructed using the vast amount of stones in the area around the home and perhaps from the creek, located down by the trees in the left of the photograph. This type of home would have been a vast improvement against the wind when compared to a log or other type of home. Notice the chimney, which would suggest a fireplace or stove of some sort was available for use inside the home for both cooking and warmth.

This is Front Street facing the Northern and Pacific Train Depot on November 15, 1886. In this photograph is the W. R. Bramble Hotel (right), most notable for the horrible case of bedbugs it had. The building was originally the James Mirrielee's Store in Dornix. When Dornix moved to Big Timber, the building was moved and became the hotel. It was also one of the first buildings in town. Farther along this block, to the left, were the Frank Bliss Saloon, Brooks Brothers Saloon, Davis House, Harrison and Anderson Livery, and William McGregor's Blacksmith Shop. Just barely visible in the background are the wagon shop of John E. Barbour and the shoe shop of John S. Solberg.

These men and their teams in 1889 are probably one of the first road crews in Big Timber. The teams are pulling "drags," which will even out the boulders in the street. This early means of paving helped keep teams and wagons from getting stuck in the mud. It also gave residents a way to try and maneuver across the street and walk above the muck.

The Busha and Bailey Hardware store, shown in 1889, was owned by C. T. Busha and his friend Joe Bailey. The men incorporated with the Clark Brothers Lumber Company to form the Montana Trading Company in 1888. Next door to the left is the Kellogg Gurney and Company, owned by H. O. Kellogg. Notice that the hardware store was also the post office at one time, as indicated by the sign out front.

As the number of merchants grew in town, so did the number of residents living in town. The first frame house in Big Timber was built and occupied by the James Mirrielee family after they moved from Dornix about 1883. Perhaps this half a house was built by someone who was short of building funds, or perhaps they just did not wish to do as much housework. In either case, half a house is better than none!

Louis Beley's Saloon and the Big Timber Liquor Company are shown in the early 1900s. The proprietor, Louis Beley, stands in front of his saloon and liquor company wearing his apron and ready for customers. In the summer of 1905, the building was constructed and owned by the Schlitz Brewing Company of Milwaukee and was called the North End Saloon. It would later be sold to Frank Beley, who in turn would sell it to his nephew Louis Beley.

McLeod Street looks north in 1921. By 1890, many of the merchants of Big Timber had shifted their establishments from Front Street to McLeod Street. As a result of this, McLeod Street became the main street of town. The street is named after W. F. McLeod, who came here from Oregon around 1882 driving a herd of 125 cattle and 200 horses. He settled here and became the first permanent homesteader of the Boulder Valley.

Shown here are the rolling foothills of the Crazy Mountains. The Homestead Act of 1862 allowed a settler to acquire ownership of 160 acres for a nominal fee, provided he resided on it continually and cultivated it for five years, or after a period of 14 months, he could purchase the acres for $1.25 each and gain title immediately. In 1905, there were approximately 41 million acres in Montana, with most of it located east of the western mountain ranges, that were available to claim and homestead under the Homestead Act of 1862. Obviously, gaining the land and subsequently owning it proved to be easier said than done.

A ranch homestead is shown in the 1900s. For many, the harsh conditions, hard work, isolation, and lack of money would prove to be too much. For others, their hard work, dedication, and perhaps a bit of luck would find them with a new life that fulfilled their expectations and perhaps their dreams. Imagine the hard work and the number of physical hours it took to make this homestead the prosperous-looking home it is. Notice the lovely and functional plants and flowers out in front and near the door. Everyone is spruced up and ready for the arrival of company.

A farmer walks behind his horse-drawn plow on May 4, 1889. In this early farming photograph taken by Clarence Farnsworth, one can see how extremely difficult and time-consuming the farming process was. Notice at the bottom of the photograph that this farmer must first turn over grass and get rid of numerous rocks before he can even think of doing any planting. Unfortunately, soil conditions were often the least of the farmers' worries. Weather would too often prove to be the farmers' undoing. Long, cold winters would lead into late springs that led into hot, dry, windy summers scarce with rain, followed by the early arrival of winter.

The addition to this homestead ranch home north of Big Timber suggests that this couple is doing well. Notice the older section has the chimney and is made of logs while the newer section is made of lumber. Piles of what appears to be scrap lumber sit near the buggy; from firewood to furniture making, every bit would have been used. In the background to the left of the home is Wormser Butte.

Two

PROGRESS AND PROSPERITY

Sheep, sheep, and more sheep are shown around 1908. This photograph by A. T. Webster shows the vast number of sheep a major ranch might have had from the late 1800s into the early 1900s. While the definition of the term "band" varies, it is widely used to describe a large amount of sheep, anywhere between 1,000 to 1,500 ewes. The first sheep arrived in the area with the first pioneers. The ranchers quickly found out that the area around Big Timber was well suited to raising sheep. It was the combination of vast acres of available grazing lands and plenty of lush native grasses.

Big Timber, Mont.

Along with the success of raising sheep, the town also saw numerous changes in the years between the late 1800s and the early 1900s. Remember that the things so easily taken for granted today would be welcome lifestyle changes. Things like electric lights would replace coal oil lamps, running water would replace a trip to the well or the river, telephones would arrive, electric refrigerators would replace the icebox, and automobiles would arrive on the scene.

Main Street looking North, Big Timber, Mont.

These bands of sheep are grazing in the snowy Boulder Mountains in August 1917. These two photographs by S. N. Lavold show the changeable weather that can occur in the mountains. This unexpected snowstorm happened over two days, August 9 and 10, 1917. The storm dropped 20 inches of snow on the unsuspecting sheep and their herders.

Sheep are being moved to the summer grazing pastures. There are approximately 1,200 sheep being moved, and it took two days to make the trip. Notice the vast amounts of snow in the month of March.

This photograph taken on July 2, 1916, shows the bridge built 60 feet above the flooded river so these sheep could cross the river and get to their summer grazing land.

Sylvester Lavold and his loyal sheepdog tend sheep on the Boulder River in 1938. It is a tribute to the many sheepherders in Big Timber's history, like Lavold, that Sweet Grass County High School's mascot is the Shepherder. They are called the Herders for short.

This sheep camp was located in the Boulder Mountain area. The shepherd would live here from early spring until fall, when the sheep were moved back to the ranch for the winter months. It was his job to protect the sheep as best he could from predators. This camp is rustic and basic but has the obvious necessities, from pots and pans hanging from the tree, to the basin on legs, to the gun. Life up in the mountains with the sheep was very isolated but also very beautiful and peaceful.

These sheep have already been sheared, which was typically done in early spring before they had their lambs. This moving camp for the herders and their supplies will be stationary once the grazing lands are reached. Notice the bands of sheep in the photograph. Also notice the traces of snow on the mountains above the sheep.

These are Big Timber sheep shearers in 1910. As the sheep population increased, so did the number of workers needed to care for all aspects of them. With the increase in jobs, the population also increased. On June 7, 1890, George M. Hatch started a new enterprise for Big Timber. He secured some land west of town near the cemetery, where he built sheds and pens. He then engaged about 25 sheep shearers to shear. The sheep ranchers would drive the sheep through to be sheared. They called these pens the Hardscrabble Pens.

Shearing pens

Big Timber Mont

These sheep shearers in action in 1910 are busy shearing three "woolies," as sheep are often called. All the sheep shearing was done by hand with a soft touch and very sharp shears. A shearer was usually paid by the piece, so speed was also a factor. Shearing is an art form, and each shearer had his own way of doing the task.

This is the last oxen team to haul wool to the wool house. In 1892, Big Timber was a major exporter of wool. The sheep ranchers actually raised one percent of the total wool for the world's use that year. By 1897, when this photograph was taken, only 102,000 pounds of wool was shipped out versus 2 million pounds shipped out in 1886. Sheep ranching was clearly on the decline.

This is the interior of the Big Timber Wool House in 1892. The bags of wool are stacked to the ceiling waiting to be sold and shipped out by train. The sleds and pull cart were used to move these very heavy bags of wool. By 1886, Big Timber was one of the largest exporters of wool in the entire world, shipping out over 2 million pounds that year alone.

Each of these stuffed bags of wool typically weighed between 300 and 400 pounds each. The wool was literally stuffed by hand into these bags to be taken to market.

Haying in Montana, Grosfield ranch.

As the available grazing lands diminished, the need for hay to feed both sheep and cattle increased. Ranchers and farmers alike naturally turned to harvesting the abundant natural grasses to feed their livestock over the winter months. These photographs show the process of stacking hay, which was the method used to store it until it was needed. The ranch in the above photograph is the Grosfield Ranch. Below is the Briggs-Ellis Ranch.

Briggs-Ellis Ranch Stacking Hay Big Timber Mont.

The first hydroelectric plant used water from the Boulder River to generate electricity. In 1905, E. O. Keppler got a license to operate a Corlis steam generator at the same site where the first hydroelectric plant was. These early linesmen are certainly ready to do their job.

In the early days, the town offered little in the way of everyday comforts. Shopping in town was not an option in the very beginning, so supplies had to be freighted in from Bozeman, 80 miles away. Lists would be made, and a four-horse team and a large wagon would make the run. A wagon usually went every six months. Some of the most sought after items were cloth, gingham, shirting, denim, and other items for making clothes; shoes and hardware items were also needed frequently. Groceries were especially requested. Staple items needed for everyday cooking were only available every six months. A mercantile like this one, Kellogg and Walbridge, would have been a very welcome addition to town.

In the early West, most frontier towns had five predictable establishments: a hotel to accommodate travelers and prospective townspeople; a saloon offering whiskey, shady ladies, and poker; a barbershop offering a two-bit haircut, a 10¢ shave, and maybe a bath if there was a bathhouse out back; a livery stable to board horses and to rent horses, wagons, and buggies; and a blacksmith to shoe horses, fix wagons, and sharpen plows.

This is Perrine's Barbershop. In July 1889, Big Timber had a female barber.

The *Big Timber Pioneer* newspaper made its debut on November 29, 1890. The paper was started by Morton Williams Hatch and Company in 1889. This building was the first printing office for the paper and was located close to the Sweet Grass County Courthouse. It would go on to have numerous owners and offices. The town reaction to the paper was positive. It said that the paper was neatly printed and a credit to both the town and Hatch. The *Big Timber Pioneer* newspaper is still printed once a week.

The Budd, Kellogg, and Vickery (known as the BK&V) General Merchandise Store must have been a welcome addition to the community. Notice the large storefront on this building. It is much taller than the rest of the building. These false fronts were built because they made the store look more impressive and gave the appearance of the store being larger than it actually was. If the gathering out front is any indication, in 1892, when this photograph was taken, this was a very popular stop in town.

When a pioneer woman would speak out about her life, it would usually include the hardships and busy life of being a wife and mother. As one woman said, "I had to leave behind many cherished and beloved items at home. I was told they would be replaced once our new home was established but they never were, there was no money for nice things." Their workload was heavy, difficult, and usually never-ending. They worked right alongside their husbands from dawn until dusk, regardless of the weather. Some took to this life and even embraced it, while others found it awful and unbearable. These ladies have managed to find the time to dress up, get together as a group, and even have their photograph taken.

With the abundance of wool in the area, the local women would spend time socializing and working with the wool. The woman on the right is carding the wool, the woman in the center is spinning the carded wool, and the woman on the left is knitting the spun wool.

The first school district was organized in 1881 at the Howie settlement, located on the lower Sweet Grass Creek. The first teacher was Lizzie Evans. When school was established in Big Timber in 1884, there were only four pupils left attending the Howie School, so school was suspended until 1889. Unfortunately, the teacher, Evans, was shot while out horseback riding one afternoon by a jealous suitor. The man was caught and hung from a cottonwood tree near Big Timber Creek. But alas, "Miss Lizzie" died from the effects of her wounds.

The students and their teacher gathered in front of the Deer Creek School in 1899. As the population both in town and in the surrounding areas grew, so did the number of families with school-age children. Notice that there are a larger number of smaller children than there are older ones. This is because once children reached an age when they could be a working asset on the family homestead they no longer attended school.

First Post Office in Central Montana – 1881
#18   KENT'S PHOTO SHOP

This early 1881 post office, while not located in the Big Timber area, would have looked like the Big Timber area post office. The first post office in Big Timber was established on May 14, 1880. It lasted until March 23, 1881. The post office would open and close many times in the years to come.

The Big Timber Post Office is pictured on Wednesday, June 1, 1910. This interior view of the post office shows the organized system for sorting the mail. The workers are women; however, most of the time, the postmaster was a man. Notice the electric lightbulbs hanging from the ceiling and the very large typewriter on the shelf on the left side of the room.

This *c.* 1910 photograph of the Big Timber Post Office, located on McLeod Street, was taken by George Kauffman.

In June 1910, Beley's Saloon was the place to go for whiskey and conversation. As one can see, the interior is well decorated with hunting trophies of all types. The proprietor, Beley, is the one in the apron.

Once the Sweet Grass County lines were drawn March 5, 1895, the need for a courthouse arose. In April 1897, a vote was taken and passed to erect a courthouse. In November 1897, the building was accepted. It cost $19,590 to build and was completed in 1898. The small building seen to the left of the courthouse is the printing office of the *Big Timber Pioneer* newspaper.

This is the interior of the courtroom in the early 1900s.

Two gentlemen clerks of the court are at work in the courthouse.

In 1913, the courthouse was used as a classroom for the freshman class of the Sweet Grass County High School.

This is a postcard of the Sweet Grass County Courthouse in 1908.

These two young boys riding on their mule on McLeod Street in 1910 have stopped in front of Egeland Boot and Shoe Shop on the right. On the left is a harness shop.

This view is looking north on McLeod Street toward the Crazy Mountains. With electric lights, telephones, and even sidewalks, the town has come a long way since November 6, 1883, when John Anderson registered Desert Claim No. 179 at the land office in Bozeman for 131.35 acres adjacent the train depot. By August 1889, the plot survey was completed for the town of Big Timber.

The c. 1800 Stone Barn was a livery, feed, sale, and stable business. There was a great need for all the types of services this business offered. Hiring a horse alone or with a buggy or wagon, boarding a horse if one was visiting or lived in town, obtaining feed for horses, and the buying and selling of horses were all important aspects of a society where the main mode of transportation was the horse.

When the automobile did arrive in the area, it went from being a novelty to a necessity in a few short years. It remained a real challenge to drive in this rugged country, however, for many more years. Regardless of the rough, rocky, and often muddy roads, everyone was always ready for an outing in the automobile, even the family dog.

An 1890s Northern Pacific Railroad work gang is seen here. The building of the railroad brought many surprises, not the least of which were the Asian work gangs that came with the railroad. Some of them stayed and called Big Timber home. They brought with them a new culture and new businesses as well. One Chinese man, Hop Sing Yim, was well thought of by the townspeople. They felt he was more cultured, wise, and more progressive than other "coolies." He owned a restaurant, grocery, and laundry. He served the most delicious bread in his establishment, the New China Café, and he generously shared the special yeast he used to make this bread rise so high with the local women. He traded his yeast for their eggs, milk, or other items, and he was very happy to do so because he wished for the townspeople to look upon him with favor.

New arrivals to town at the train depot are met by promoters of the new Glasston area. Notice the automobiles lined up and ready to take the new arrivals to see the area, which was north of town near Glasston Lake. The company was called Glasston-Lindsay. Many people would come from the East to see what the western experience was all about. For about $30, one could purchase a train ticket from Chicago. Unfortunately for the promoters, the town never really took off, and today only the lake remains.

E. B. Clark, E. O. Clark, C. T. Busha, and John Asbury are the men seated from left to right on this railroad handcar. These men were all instrumental in the progress of Big Timber and the surrounding areas. They were financially involved in banks, businesses, and the wool industry. Asbury was the town's first mayor.

The Big Timber National Bank was started in 1891 with a capital of $50,000.

This is the interior of the Big Timber National Bank in 1892. The cashier in the front window is J. A. Hall. John F. Asbury is in the second cashier window. J. A. Hall organized the bank, which was established in 1891.

This is a copy of a bank note from 1906–1907 from the Big Timber National Bank. The bank was originally organized by J. A. Hall in 1891.

This ranch was owned by the Reverend Andrew Wormser and his wife, Anna (Holdemaker), who arrived in the area from the Netherlands in 1895. He organized the Holland Irrigation Canal Company north of Big Timber at the base of the Crazy Mountains. The company was made up of workers, most of whom had originally come from the Netherlands with little else but the promise of a good job and a piece of land to farm once the canal was finished. The company men used horses, scrappers, and hand ploughs to dig a large ditch or canal off of Big Timber Creek in hopes of irrigating the fields in the areas off the creek. Reverend Wormser's residence was built near the creek. It was a large home with several lovely features, like hardwood floors, leaded-glass windows, native stone work, and several fireplaces. The carriage house located to the left of the house had living quarters upstairs for the servants. It still stands today and is used as a private residence.

Dr. Albert P. O'Leary's Hospital opened its doors on June 1, 1913. The new hospital could hold 12 patients at a time. The old hospital was lost to a fire. While this hospital would originally belong to Dr. O'Leary, it would be run by different practitioners in the years to come.

Dr. Lindsay Baskett (left) and Dr. E. F. McCann sit together in Dr. Baskett's office in June 1917. Notice the physician's bag and the examining table on the right of the photograph. Prior to the arrival of a physician, Elizabeth Meadow Jones, a trained nurse and the only one in the area, would come from Livingston by train, usually by handcar.

This is the Patterson Grocery and Hardware Store around 1914. Just think: residents could purchase bananas and nails all at once. Notice all the interesting items in this store. They certainly made good use of every inch of space.

The first meat shop that opened in town was Dan Hogan's Meat Shop. This meat shop looks quite elegant, with the stocked cases of meat selections along with the fancy hooks with sausage on the back wall. Notice the scales with weights, the large cash register, the spittoon, and even an electric fan on the counter. The hunting trophies are quite interesting as well. Even the ceiling light has a shade on it.

The need for a Sunday school arose, so Ellen DeWitt Hatch formed one. This Episcopal church was the first church in town built of native stone and was erected in 1895 at a cost of approximately $2,500. The building to the right is the parsonage. Episcopal church services are still held at St. Mark's Episcopal Church every Sunday.

The family living in this later example of a frame house certainly seems to be enjoying their home, even the family cat.

When gold was discovered on the Upper Boulder River in 1879, a small army of men swarmed up the mountain slopes and quickly filed mining claims. Many camps consisted of just a tent for protection, while the lucky ones may have had a picket pin log cabin like this one, complete with a pair of snow skis.

Picket Pin   Sweet Grass Co.

This was the letter sent to the stockholders of the Standard Mining Company in 1903. The Standard Mine was located up the Boulder in Contact.

TO THE STOCK-HOLDERS OF THE STANDARD MINING COMPANY:

COWLES MINING CAMP

This is an aerial view of the Cowles Mining Camp. By 1891, the grand mining rush had begun. The Independence Mining Company was running full blast in 1892–1893. In 1892, the camp had a population of 500 or more. In the summer of 1893, a 10-foot cut revealed a face of white quartz that glistened with gold. They called this the Minnie Mine, and it caused mass hysteria and excitement and a general stampeding in all directions into the Boulder Mountains. Mining for various minerals, including copper, nickel, gold, chrome, and palladium, has come and gone through the years. In the mountains nearby, the Stillwater Mining Company continues its Boulder mining operations today.

The year 1893 saw both the prosperity and the decline of the mining phenomenon in the area. However, because of the influx of people to the area, by the spring of 1893, Big Timber had more residents than ever before. The economy of the town would be helped greatly by the miners who had outfitted themselves with supplies before leaving town to go and try their luck at striking it rich.

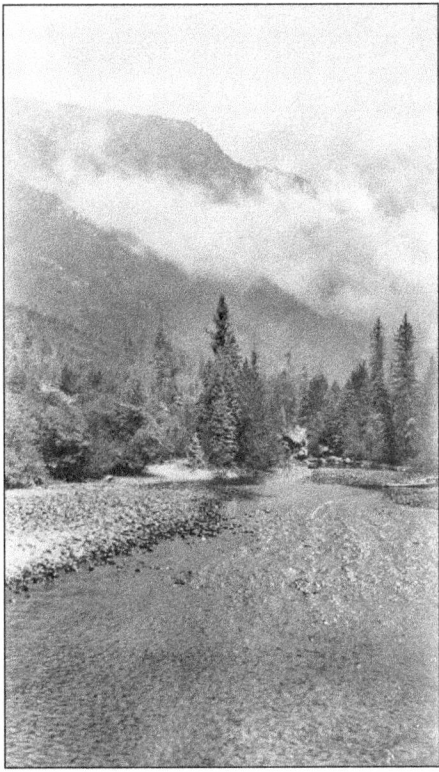

A work crew with road-grading equipment works on a road below.

The Boulder Valley proved to be a very fertile place. In 1885, the first irrigation was started, and by 1887, the first seeds had been sown and harvested. Approximately 9,000 bushels were threshed in the valley, all by a horse-powered machine owned by Bert Wheaton. In the summer of 1896, it was estimated that there were 15,000 to 18,000 head of cattle, almost 2,000 head of horses, and 35,000 to 40,000 sheep. This steam-powered tractor that would come along later would certainly be a welcome addition to the team.

Three

TRAGEDY STRIKES

The Northern Pacific Railroad westbound No. 5 stopped at the depot in this A. T. Webster photograph. On Friday, March 13, 1908, a spark blown from a locomotive stopped at the depot started a fire in some rubbish near the stockyards. The exceedingly high winds that day helped to quickly spread the sparks and embers to various locations across the entire town. The cinders immediately ignited whatever they landed on—grass, buildings, rubbish, homes, anything burnable. Before it was all over, one-third of the entire town would be completely destroyed.

The first residence to be destroyed was the home of Fred Severance. Next to go was the Liebel Brothers West Side Livery business; fortunately, all the horses and most of the contents of the business were saved. From the livery stable, the fire spread to the Montana Hotel, and within minutes, the entire block was aflame.

By now, the Big Timber Volunteer Fire Brigade had more than it could possibly handle. There was just too much fire in such a short amount of time, and thanks to the wind, it was spreading faster than they could possibly keep up with. Luckily, the Livingston Fire Brigade showed up on a train about this time to help. They were able to help contain the blaze on that side of town.

54

As the blaze continued, Perrine's Barbershop and the Club Saloon were badly damaged but saved. At the same time, the Carrol Block and all business houses in that block, including S. R. Dillion's Horse's Home Barn and Dillion's residence were reduced to ashes. Two very valuable horses were lost also.

The fire then rapidly spread east. A total of 23 business establishments were totally destroyed including this one, the Dier Browning Mercantile Company, a much-loved mercantile that not only carried everyday items but exotic silks and other items from around the globe.

The Bell Telephone Office, the Chinese Laundry, and Citizens State Bank were also completely lost. This building is the temporary bank that was set up after the fire. Around it can be seen the total devastation.

There were 21 homes destroyed, with several of these families losing not only their business but their home as well. It was a devastating loss. There were also many homes that suffered major damage. The electric service and phone service were in ruins.

On Friday afternoon, even before the smoke had cleared, a mass town meeting was held and plans were put into motion to help those who were in need. By nightfall, thanks to the selfless efforts of the entire community and especially the heroic efforts of the relief committee, everyone had a place to stay.

Most of the losses were not covered by insurance. The Northern Pacific Railroad admitted negligence and eventually settled all the claims made on them. But the rebuilding process was very slow and time consuming. The townspeople also petitioned the railroad company to move the stockyards to the east side of town because they considered them a fire hazard. This A. T. Webster photograph looking north toward the Crazy Mountains shows what was left on McLeod Street. The large brick building on the right side of the street is the Grand Hotel, while the building across the street on the left is the Fair Department Store. Also notice the train at the end of the street.

FRIDAY MAR 13 08 BIGTIMBER MONT,

While the fire of 1908 was clearly the worst one to date, fires were not an uncommon occurrence in and around Big Timber. There were two fires in town in 1890. A fire in 1893 destroyed (thankfully) the bedbug-ridden Bramble Hotel, and a wildfire in 1894 burned parts of two ranches north of town. The building remains on the left are the Dier Browning Building, while the Opera House (the building in the center of the photograph) is still standing.

Birds eye view of burned section Big Timber.

This bird's-eye view of the burned section of the town allows one to see the vast amount of devastation that occurred that unlucky Friday the 13th.

58

Four

HOME SWEET HOME

The largest street running from the lower left corner to the center of the right side in this aerial view of Big Timber is McLeod Street. The rebuilding of the town after the 1908 fire gave some businesses and homeowners as well the opportunity to not only rebuild but in some cases to enlarge homes and businesses. Many new businesses also came to town during those years. The population increased, and life once again settled into a routine.

This is the 1908 confirmation class at the Scandinavian Evangelical Lutheran Church.

This is the 1908 confirmation class with the entire congregation standing in front of the Scandinavian Evangelical Lutheran Church.

The Sweet Grass High School graduating class of 1909 included, from left to right, Estelle Prevost, Selmer Solberg, Charles Busha, Ronald Halverson, and Ingrid Halverson.

High School, Big Timber, Mont.

This is a postcard made from an A. T. Webster photograph of the Sweet Grass High School. The high school was completed in 1905, and the first class to complete a four-year course of study and graduate was the class of 1906. The Sweet Grass County Courthouse, the building with the tower, is visible behind the school, as are the Crazy Mountains.

In 1901, the library started as a shelf of books in a local store. By April 4, 1910, the town was talking about an actual library. By 1911, there was an actual library with 13,000 volumes housed in the town hall. The first librarian was Lena Clark. About this time, the town approached industrialist and library patron Andrew Carnegie in the hopes of securing funding for a new library building. Carnegie agreed to provide $7,500 with a stipulation that the town provide the site where the building would be constructed and set aside taxes to support the library services. These same stipulations were made for all the Carnegie Libraries. The architectural firm of Link and Haire built the library in 1914; it embraces the classical revival elements of design that became popular after being used at the 1893 Columbian Exposition in Chicago. The river rock used on the bottom of the building is local native rock. Once the library was built, it stayed open evenings in order to offer people an alternative diversion to a saloon or a pool hall.

The Big Timber Grade School's students and staff members gathered in front of the school in 1905.

This is a classroom of students and their teacher at the Big Timber Grade School.

An assembly of the student body was held at the Sweet Grass High School in 1916.

Big Timber, Mont

The Fair Department Store in 1902 was a complete and elegant department store. The building was constructed in 1890 by G. M. Hatch. The store was established by C. A. Caulkins.

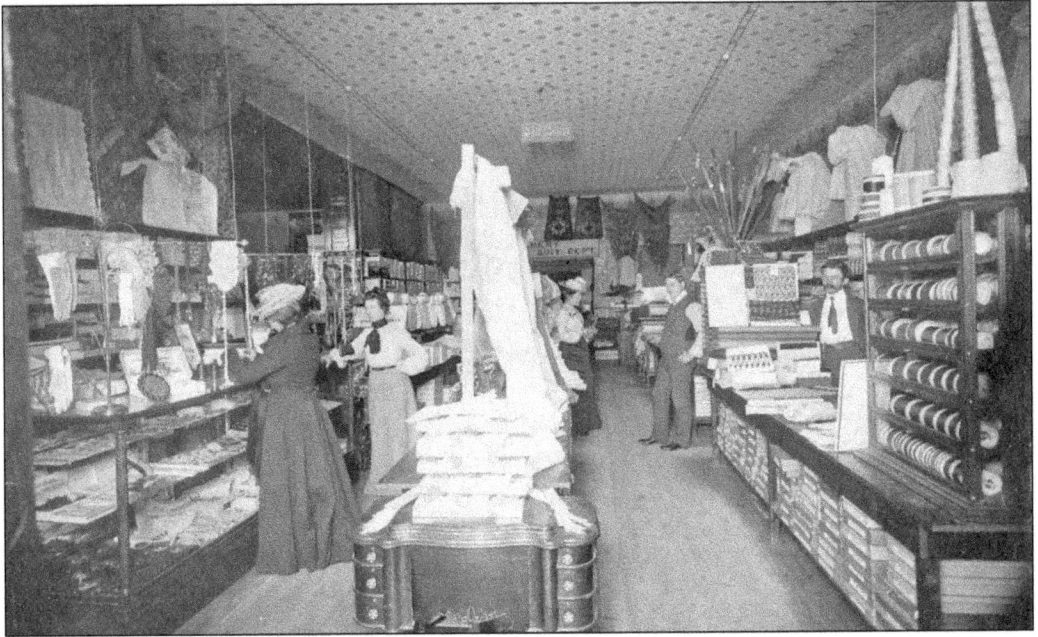

This interior photograph of the Fair Department Store in 1902 shows at least two separate departments. It appears that the ladies' accessories department is on the left side of the store, and the dry goods department is on the right. Notice some of the items for sale in each of the different departments—like gloves, hankies, lace collars, ribbons, and fabrics. The sign in the back offers an idea as to what departments are located through the doorway.

This interior view of the Fair Department Store shows the millinery, cloak, and suit departments. This part of the store was located through the back doorway that was visible in the previous photograph.

John F. Asbury, his wife, and two daughters lived in this home on McLeod Street. Asbury was a businessman and the beloved first mayor of Big Timber. Notice the fence in front of the house; it consists of 155 elk antlers. The inside of the home had bird's-eye maple paneling, hardwood parquet floors, and a Tiffany chandelier in the dining room.

(Elizabeth) (Dorothy)
Gussie and Sister with Girlie in the Sleigh.
Jan. 1912

In January 1912, there was a considerable amount of snow on the ground. The Asbury girls, Elizabeth ("Gussie") and Dorothy ("Sister"), seem to have found a delightful way to enjoy the winter weather. Here they are bundled up against the cold taking a ride in their sleigh, being pulled by their horse named Girlie. They have stopped in front of their home to have their picture taken.

In this snowy scene, one can just get a glimpse of the home that belonged to the Asbury family through the snow-covered trees in January 1912. John Asbury was a true pillar of the community. He was the first mayor and served from December 1902 until May 1913. In his first four years, he bonded the city for $40,000 worth of waterworks. Electric lights came to town in 1906, and the first cement sidewalks were put into place in 1912. He served for 11 years. He was well respected, and it was generally believed that he always had the city's best interest at heart when making decisions. Asbury became ill shortly after he left office, so he traveled to Kirksville, Missouri, to a sanatorium, where he died of pneumonia in December 1915; he was 51 years old. Mrs. Asbury was actually on her way to see him when he suddenly died. She was so overcome with grief that she also became seriously ill and went to a sanatorium away from home, where she died in November 1916. The now orphaned Asbury girls, Gussie and Sister, had remained at home in Big Timber in order to finish their last year of high school.

The Webster family went on an outing in town, and even the dog came along. Meeting and greeting friends and family was almost an everyday occurrence when living in town, as most townspeople walked to get where they were going.

The house on the left with the fancy turret was the home of J. A. Hall and his wife, Emetine (Marks), and his two daughters, Helen and Irene. J. A. Hall was a well-respected businessman in the community. He was responsible for organizing the Big Timber National Bank. In 1893, he became interested in sheep ranching and at one point, he owned the largest sheep ranch in Montana. He was also president of the Midland Coal and Lumber Company. He was a man of substantial character and a true supporter of the growing city of Big Timber. The home to the right was that of John Asbury.

The young people, named Earl, Billie, and Nellie are visiting on the front porch. Conversation and visiting was a popular pastime. It was not only easy to do, but it did not cost anything to do it.

In 1909, this large home, believed to belong to the Grosfield family, was located across from the Sweet Grass County Courthouse.

Sometimes even the most basic chores turned into an adventure. This c. 1936 couple is braving a snowstorm to ride to town and buy some groceries.

The train depot is certainly a busy place on this day in 1911.

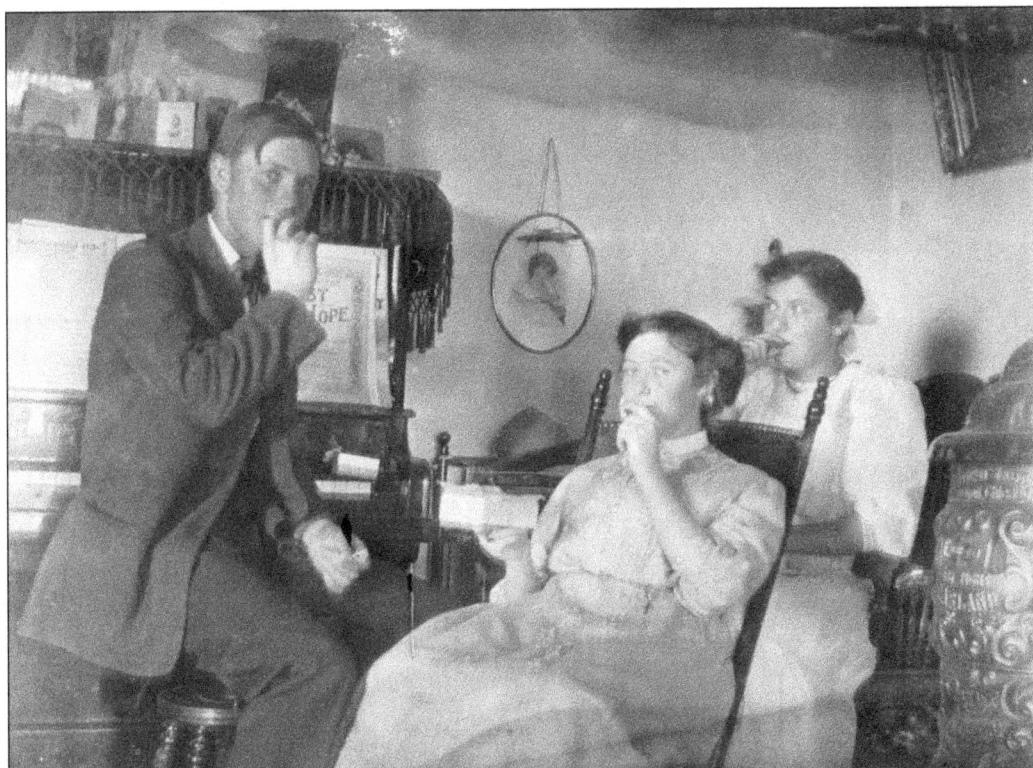

This family is enjoying what looks to be a box of sweets together. The piano would also provide a source of family fun.

In 1920, the 19th Amendment was passed, giving women across the United States the right to vote. In the state of Montana, the women were already allowed to vote, having been given that right in 1914. By 1916, Montana had elected the first female member of Congress. Her name was Jeannette Rankin, elected to the House of Representatives just two years after the women of Montana were given the right to vote. How proud these Big Timber women must have felt when that happened, especially since they had marched right here in town for their right to vote.

These schoolchildren are gathered in front of Wild Rose School, the rural school that was built in 1920. The school was located north of Big Timber on Big Timber Creek.

The Wild Rose School, pictured here, was located north of Big Timber and classes were taught for 32 continuous years.

This group of students and their teacher are from the mid-1900s, as one can tell from their clothing. Even today, rural schools continue be a part of the Sweet Grass County School system.

These young men dressed in their uniforms are World War I inductees. This induction took place in front of the Carnegie Library. The home visible on the right is the first frame house built in Big Timber by the James Mirrielee family.

These gentlemen are World War II inductees waiting to board the bus that will take them to Butte, Montana, on August 17, 1942.

The U.S. Forest Service came about in 1905 as a result of the government feeling the need to protect and regulate the forests. Up until this time, people were free to extract lumber, minerals, water, and other resources from the area, which often caused major damage, especially to the watersheds. The U.S. government believed that if the devastation continued, there would be nothing left of the forest reserves, so the U.S. Forest Service was established.

The first ranger arrived in the area in 1903. His name was Harry S. Kaufman. He was 20 years old when he applied and received the ranger position on the Main Boulder. He built the Main Boulder Ranger Station seen here. The station is located up the Main Boulder Road in the Gallatin National Forest. Today this cabin has been lovingly and authentically restored, and it is open to visitors in the summer months.

In 1909, Harry enlarged his one-room cabin in the hopes of someday having a wife and family. In 1911, he married Coral McKnight. Eventually, a son, Harry Kaufman Jr., was born. Harry Jr. is two years old here, and he is standing on a chair on the screened porch of the ranger station looking at a friend. A few years later, Harry Jr. would be joined by a sister named Betty. The family would live together in this cozy cabin for many years.

The ranger had many responsibilities and a vast amount of space to watch over. In the early spring, Harry was responsible for overseeing the sheep grazing allotments. He would be responsible for counting all the sheep in each allotment to be sure the correct number were on each permitted area. Another one of his jobs was to maintain communications with other areas of his jurisdiction, as well as keep in contact with other locations. He was expected to keep in touch with the town of Big Timber, his superior officer in Livingston, and the Meyers Gulch Ranger Station. To accomplish this, Harry strung and maintained miles and miles of telephone lines across the rugged countryside. It was a continuous job; once he finished checking all the lines, it was time to start all over again. In this photograph, Harry is seen making a telephone call using the "spike box," which was located in the area called "telephone meadows," while his companions wait patiently. Notice the thick case the telephone is in. This is to protect it from the elements such as high winds, rain, snow, or perhaps even a curious bear.

This is the main switchboard for the telephone system located in the small office of the ranger station. Each of these lines goes to a different location, and each line had its own set of bells so operators could tell which line was ringing. Harry would use these phone lines for both emergencies and routine purposes. One could also guess he might even use the one from the field to call and check on Coral and the children, especially if he was out in the wilderness for several days or even weeks at a time. Harry remained the ranger until 1941, when ill health forced him to retire to Livingston, Montana.

A threshing crew harvesting hay is using a steam-driven piece of equipment.

Workers harvest hay using horses, wagons, and even an automobile. The tents suggest a makeshift camp set up to house the workers.

McLeod Street, facing north toward the Crazy Mountains, is dug up as natural gas lines are installed. The Grand Hotel is on the right, and the building across the street once housed the Fair Department Store.

Sidewalks come to a section of town in 1912.

This collage of four photographs was used by Citizen's Bank for a centennial calendar. The top two are street views, the bottom view is the Crazy Mountains, and the center photograph is the Sweet Grass County Courthouse.

Five

A FIDDLE, A BOW, AND A DO-SI-DO

Social life typically centered on work, church, or school without regard to whether someone lived in or out of town. These sheep shearers are relaxing after a busy day of backbreaking work. They all look exhausted, but one gentleman seems to have enough energy left to kick up his heels and do a little jig.

Automobiles provided a fun activity for those who had them or had access to them. Although road conditions could prove frustrating, it certainly did not seem to limit their appeal. On August 1, 1915, private automobiles were allowed in Yellowstone Park. The speed limit was 12 miles per hour, and just like in Big Timber, "teams" (horses and wagons) always had the right-of-way.

If this photograph is any indication, it looks like everyone enjoyed an outing in the automobile, even this bear.

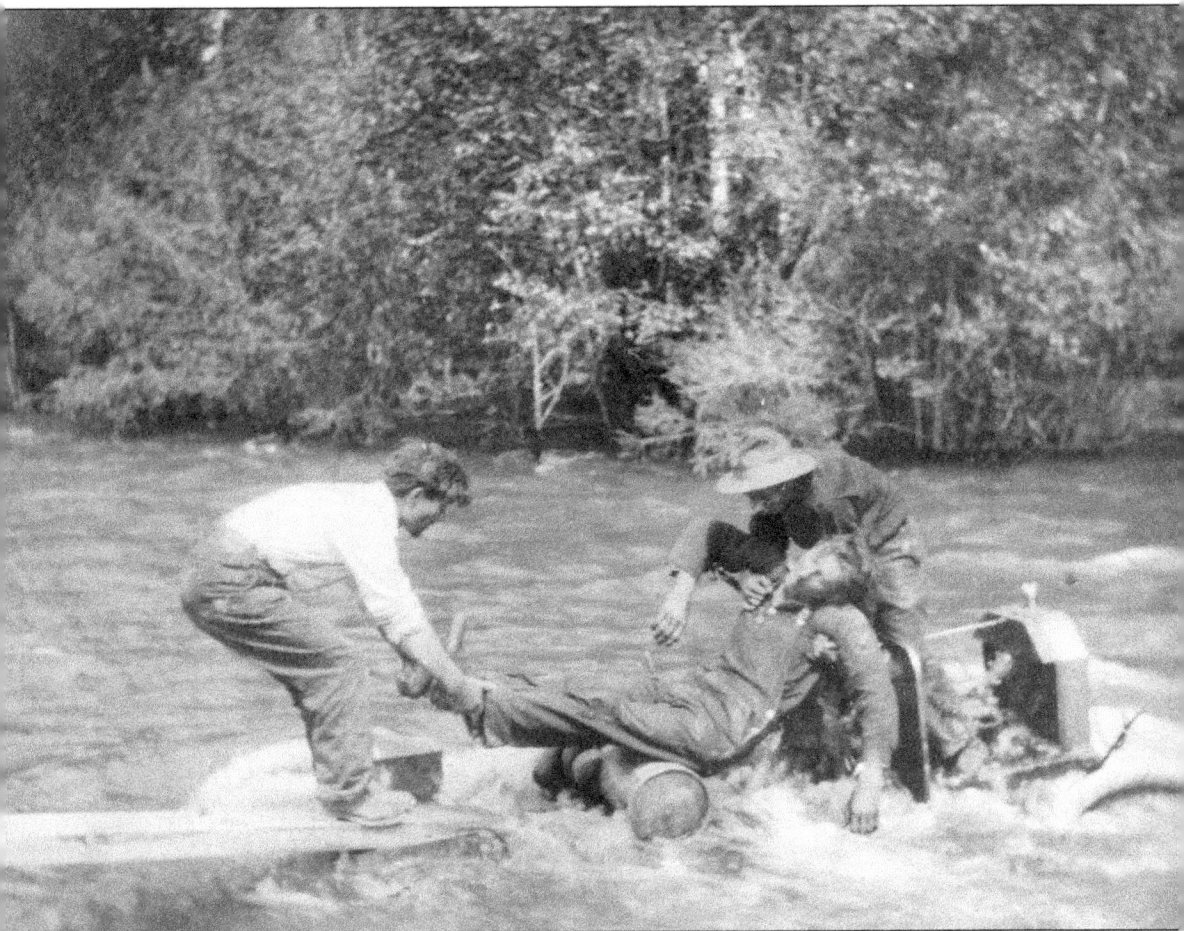

Was it road conditions or driver conditions that caused this motorist to lose control of his automobile, drive off the bridge, and end up in the river?

The circus comes to town. These elephants are standing in front of the train cars that brought their circus to Big Timber.

A circus would not be complete without a parade to announce its arrival. This pony-pulled chariot rolls down McLeod Street while townspeople watch.

The circus band rides down McLeod Street.

Here is the circus dog and donkey act. The Grand Hotel is in the background.

Did someone mention dogs? This circus wagon is certainly overflowing with them.

Another popular pastime was horse racing. It provided entertainment in numerous ways: raising the racehorses, watching the races, wagering on the races, and discussing the races both before and after they were run.

These Big Timber Grade School students are playing on the seesaw in 1929.

The same group of grade-school students lined up for a photograph on this wooden slide in 1929.

Happy May Day! A group of students are performing the traditional maypole dance in 1929.

WOMANS CLUB SKATING RINK - BIG TIMBER, MONT.

This skating pond was provided by the Big Timber Women's Club in 1929. Skating was a fun pastime for children. Also note the girl with her sled in the photograph. Children spent a great deal of time playing, especially outside, in 1929.

From its opening day to the present day, the Grand Hotel remains a town gathering place. Through the years, the Grand has boasted of having steam heat, electric lights, indoor plumbing, and telephone service in every room. The rates in those early days ranged from $2 to $3 per day. Today the Grand continues to be the place to meet and greet and share a meal. It is also listed on the National Register of Historic Places.

In 1920, music was a pastime enjoyed by adults and children. Dressed up and holding her violin, this young girl certainly looks pleased.

The Opera House was built by O. M. Lamphear for the owner, W. J. Hannah, in 1902. It opened July 11, 1902, with a performance by the Logan Orchestra of Billings, Montana. The Opera House or Auditorium, as it was most commonly called, was constructed entirely by Big Timber labor. The building was "virtually fireproof" because of the unique construction materials used, such as concrete and metal. While the building was never aesthetically appealing, it was well used and enjoyed by many. The plays, musicals, comedy shows, concerts, and even vaudeville shows were all immensely popular, and most played to full houses. The Auditorium was vast in size; it could seat 400 on the main floor and 100 in the balcony. It also had the ability to move all of the seating to the sides of the building, and the stage could be lifted 10 feet off the ground, creating a large open space. In fact, when cleared, the main floor area was so large that one of the Auditorium's last uses was as practice space for a newly formed boys' basketball team. At that point, the school did not have a gymnasium.

In January 1928, there was plenty of snow for this dog sled team. Waiting outside the Opera House or Auditorium, this team is ready to brave those vast amounts of snow. While the climate of the area was considered arid, which means mild and dry in the winter, it still received large amounts of snow on occasion. Due to the popularity of the shows at the Auditorium, it appears even a large snowfall could not keep these folks away.

A dog sled team waits at the ready in front of the West Side Livery, which was located across Hoopee Street from the Auditorium. The Sweet Grass County Courthouse is visible in the background.

Packhorses make a stop while on an elk hunt up the Boulder Mountain near Independence. This photograph was taken by S. N. Lavold.

In this stereopticon photograph, a cattle branding was a working social event. Those not participating are watching at the fence, and when the work is finished, everyone will share a meal together. Today brandings that take place in the area remain much the same.

The Montana Incubator Company float is in what appears to be a c. 1900 Fourth of July parade. Notice the two little girls in their pretty dresses and hats on the sidewalk between the second and third floats, as well as the little boys in their suits with knickers and hats in front of the first float.

A parade on McLeod Street draws plenty of spectators.

The John Deere Company advertises with a float on McLeod Street.

These uniformed and armed cavalry soldiers are flying the colors and marching in formation during an early Fourth of July parade as they pass the Ross Dier Mercantile Company on the left.

The Big Timber Municipal Band is pictured in a park having a concert c. 1940.

The Big Timber Cornet Band gathered together on July 4, 1903.

This snowslide occurred in 1921. It happened up the Boulder above Clydehurst near Speculator Creek. Ben Fleming, an early resident of the Main Boulder area, was killed. (Photograph by J. Nordby.)

The searchers look for Ben Fleming. Fleming was found after an extensive search not far from where his dogs had last been seen before the slide. He was found about 9 inches below the surface of the snow, and he was holding two steel traps. (Photograph by J. Nordby.)

In this photograph of the search team that found Fleming, the gentleman on the far right is John Nordby, the photographer of this and the last two images. Several years after this event occurred, Nordby himself would perish in a snowslide in this same area.

Though not technically in Sweet Grass County, Hunters Hot Springs Resort certainly played a part in the history of the area. The resort was located on the north side of the Yellowstone River 2 miles west of what is now Springdale, which is located 13 miles west of Big Timber. Hunters Hot Springs was named for Dr. Hunter from Virginia. It was said his father was a lineal descendant of Pocahontas. In February 1870, he built a log cabin at the hot springs in spite of repeated Native American encounters and attacks. The soldiers from Fort Ellis came to help. But in the end, Dr. Andrew Jackson Hunter would allow the Native Americans to use the hot springs and peace prevailed. Dr. Hunter died in Bozeman in 1894, but the springs would go on to have several owners, also doctors, as well as a full staff of physicians through the years. During the 1890s, a large frame hotel was built and the railroad brought lots of guests from around the globe to drink and bathe in the warm waters of the healing mineral springs. This sketch of the resort shows it during its heyday; the train depot is bustling with the arrival of visitors, and the resort sits across the river looking grand and inviting. A 1932 fire would take a huge toll on most of the resort, including "The Plunge," the large indoor mineral pool. The resort was rebuilt but not on such a grand scale. The plunge was recovered and remained open to the public until the mid-1970s. Today the area is a privately owned cattle ranch.

The history of rodeo in Big Timber is a simple one: work hard and play harder. The men of the area got together to see who was the best at roping and riding. Oftentimes it was not even an organized event. A rancher would bring a herd of wild horses through town, and those who were interested would gather to see who could "break 'em" the best.

LEO J CREMER OWNER OF THE FAMOUS CREMER STRING OF BUCKING HORSES. (DOUBLEDAY)

Through the years, the sport became more organized with the help of this gentleman, local stock producer Leo J. Cremer Sr., shown here on one of his favorite horses, Pronto.

Leo J. Cremer, Big Timber, Montana
(28th Year as Rodeo Producer)

**The World's Largest
Rodeo Producer**
from
**The Largest Rodeo and
Livestock Ranch**

1953 Season

Miles City, Montana	June 26-28
Mandan, North Dakota	July 3-5
Calgary, Canada (Brahma Bulls)	July 6-11
Nampa, Idaho (Snake River Stampede)	July 14-18
Ogden, Utah (Pioneer Days)	July 21-25
Great Falls, Montana	
(North Montana State Fair)	Aug. 3-8
Colorado Springs, Colo. (Pikes Peak or Bust)	Aug. 4-8
Billings, Montana (Midland Empire Fair)	Aug. 11-15
Casper, Wyoming (Central Wyoming Fair)	Aug. 12-15
Des Moines, Iowa (Iowa State Fair)	Sept. 4-7
Pueblo, Colo. (Colorado State Fair)	Sept. 7-10
Omaha, Neb. (Ak-Sar-Ben)	Sept. 25-Oct. 4
Chicago, Ill. (International Amphitheatre)	Oct. 9-18

NOTE: Other dates pending.

Leo J. Cremer Sr. spearheaded the efforts to organize rodeo in Big Timber for many years. His efforts started as early as 1925. This flyer shows all the dates of rodeos around the country for the 1953 rodeo season and a photograph of Cremer on horseback. Unfortunately, this same year, Leo J. Cremer Sr. died in an automobile accident. He was 62 years old.

In this photograph, Leo J. Cremer Sr. actively participates in a rodeo event of his own. Here he is seen "bulldogging" at a rodeo in Forsyth, Montana. This photograph was taken by R. R. Doubleday.

100

The Cremer Rodeos had all the traditional rodeo acts and featured lots of other thrilling and spectacular events. These included trick riders, stunt riders, and extraordinary ropers. Seated on his horse Pronto, Leo J. Cremer Sr. poses with a group of Native Americans in complete dress, including full feather headdresses, hand-decorated vests, and handmade exotic jewelry. There are tepees set up in the background.

Leo Cremer Sr. poses with his friends, a rodeo clown and a very large bull.

An early photograph features spectators seated in the grandstands at the Big Timber Fairgrounds. While rodeo may have started out small, by 1959, the Big Timber Rodeo was billed as the largest one-day rodeo in the Northwest.

Bertha Cremer, the wife of Leo Cremer Sr., sits on her horse.

This Cremer Ranch, known as the F. D. Ranch, was the home of Leo Cremer Jr. and his wife, Emma Gale Wilcox. They had a son named George. Today many Cremer family members still live and ranch in the Big Timber area.

Women participated in rodeo events as well, as seen in this early photograph of a girls' relay race taking place at an early ranch rodeo in Big Timber.

This group of rodeo women from Butte, Montana, would have been typical of the type of women seen at most rodeos. Today women continue to be very active participants in rodeo events such as barrel racing and roping around the country.

Six

THE MORE IT CHANGES, THE MORE IT STAYS THE SAME

Stunning scenic vistas like this one have kept many visitors returning to the area time and time again, and some have even decided to make it their second home. There are many similar views around the area that have visually remained the same for hundreds of years.

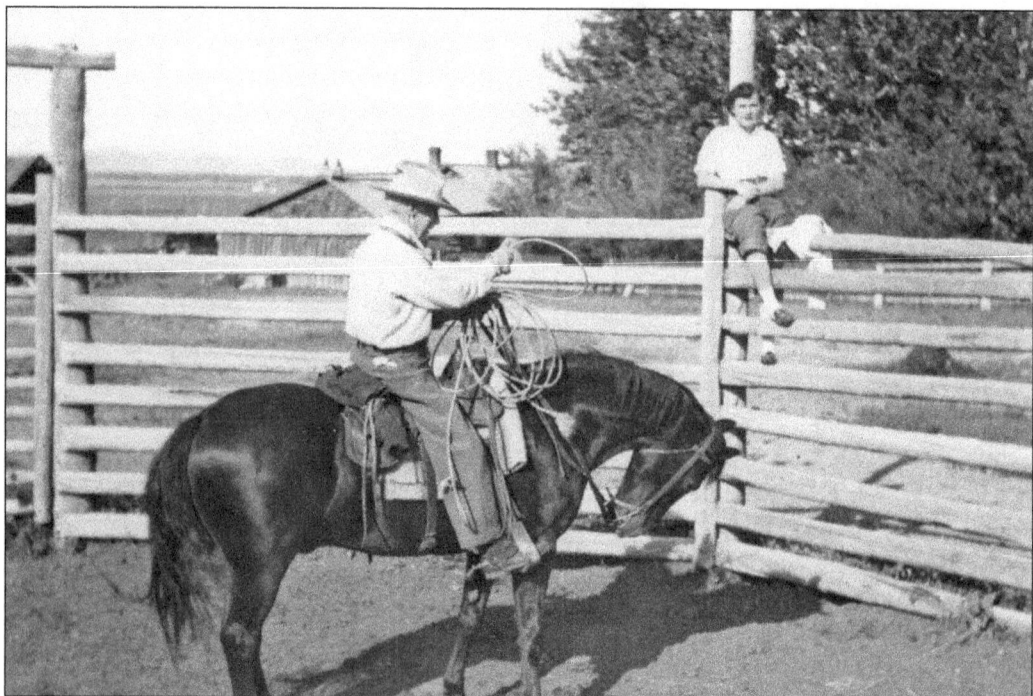

The dude ranch experience started right here in this area when the first dude ranch in the West opened on the east side of the Crazy Mountains. There are still dude ranches in the area, and they continue to be popular vacation destinations.

RETURNING FROM THE TRAIL. MAIN LODGE, CRAZY MOUNTAINS
BRANNIN RANCH, MELVILLE, MONTANA.

These "dudes" are saddled up and ready to ride. These are guests at the Brannin Dude Ranch, located north of Big Timber near Melville, Montana. Today the ranch, which is known as the Sweet Grass Ranch, is still operated as a dude ranch by the Carroccia and Dringman families. It was placed on the National Register of Historic Places.

This beautiful log hunting lodge was part of the Boulder Lodge, which is located near Contact south of Big Timber. The guests at this lodge came mostly for the outstanding hunting and fishing opportunities this wilderness area provided.

A log guest cabin is nestled in a meadow at the Boulder Lodge.

A dude ranch tucked into this scenic mountain area shows the separate guest cabins and the main buildings.

Located in a beautifully lush spot in the Boulder Mountain area, the Old Kaintuck Camp was a beloved dude ranch vacation destination. This charmingly quaint building was the main ranch house.

The tables are set, the plates are in place, and the flowers are on the table. The main dining hall at Old Kaintuck is ready and waiting for the guests to arrive for supper. The guest cabins were separate, but most activities were to be enjoyed as a group, especially dining, when meals would be served family style.

"Club Room"
Old Kaintuck Camp,
Big Timber, Mont.

While horseback riding took up the majority of time during the day, in the evenings, guests were encouraged to enjoy the company of other guests in the Club Room. Here guests could sit and visit, play cards, read a book, or just enjoy the fireplace.

This couple may be Mr. and Mrs. Walter Aller, the proprietors of Old Kaintuck. In 1947, the Allers decided that the name Old Kaintuck was not entirely suitable for a Montana dude ranch, so they changed the name to the Boulder River Ranch. Notice their riding apparel: the lady is in britches and the gentleman is wearing a necktie. Today the ranch is privately owned and no longer a dude ranch.

Standing on this unique log bridge, in 1928, looks like a fun way to enjoy the sights and sounds of the Boulder River.

Falls of the Boulder River, from Canyon Bottom,
South of Big Timber, Mont.

This is a postcard of Natural Bridge Falls, which is located 25 miles south of Big Timber on the Main Boulder. During high water, the river would flow over the top, creating a 105-foot waterfall into a pool at the base of the cliff. The water then makes its way through a narrow canyon, with some walls along the route reaching a height of 100 feet. When the water was low, it would flow through a "hole" in the top of the falls, creating the "natural bridge" across the falls. Today the natural bridge at the top of the falls no longer exists, having been worn away by water over the years. Regardless of that fact, the Falls continues to be a popular and lovely destination for both visitors and residents alike.

These visitors are viewing the Natural Bridge Falls from the bottom, near the pool.

Even in winter, the Natural Bridge Falls still remain quite a scenic sight to behold.

Fly fishermen with their fishing rods and reels are pictured in the area sometime before 1905.

Sometime before 1905, fishermen found this bridge to be a favorite spot for enjoying the sport. Fishing, especially fly-fishing, continues to gain in popularity for visitors and residents alike.

114

Hunting has a long history in this area. What started as a means of obtaining food has evolved into a popular sport among residents and visitors. These hunters and their bird dog have had a successful day of hunting grouse.

In the early 1900s, some of the ladies in the area formed the Big Timber Women's Bicycle Club. Bicycles first showed up in the area in the late 1800s, and despite the atrocious road conditions, they were an enjoyable pastime. Of course, the roads were only part of the total frustration a person might experience when riding a bicycle in the early 1900s—rough terrain, unpredictable bicycle tires, steep hills—and if those items were not enough, imagine riding in a long skirt, as these ladies are doing. The fun and novelty must have outweighed all of the other issues because not only does the club have numerous members, but most of them seem to be smiling in this photograph.

The Bull Moose Campaign stopped in Big Timber before October 1912. Pres. Theodore (he actually hated being called "Teddy") Roosevelt helped name his second campaign by responding to reporters, "I'm fit as a Bull Moose," when asked if he was physically ready to take the office of the president again. President Roosevelt (left) and Fletcher Maddox (right) stand on the back of the train stopped at the Big Timber Depot.

Leo J. Cremer Sr. (left) sits on horseback with Roy Rogers (right), who is sitting on his famous horse, Trigger. Many famous people have visited Big Timber and the surrounding areas. Gene Autry was a good friend of Cremer's; in fact, Autry purchased Cremer Rodeo Productions when Cremer died. Other famous visitors include rodeo photographer Ralph Russell Doubleday, Tom Mix, Slim Pickens, and Calamity Jane, who, rumor has it, started a tavern up the Boulder Mountain in 1882.

Rodeo "bronc" riding can still be seen today in Big Timber. The rodeo comes to town every summer at the end of June and is held at the Big Timber Fairgrounds.

The Sweet Grass County Fair was held at the Sweet Grass County Fairgrounds in 1908. This photograph was taken by A. T. Webster.

The view on this postcard is an outing to the Sweet Grass County Fair in the early 1900s. It looks like young and old alike are going to the fair. Notice the fashion styles for both men and women. Even the young child (between the two men) is well turned out for this outing to the fair.

Ranching and raising cattle continue to be the major sources of income for many people working in this area. These men on horseback are moving cattle to a different pasture location via the road. This is not an infrequent sight even today.

A roundup of cattle is taking place. When roundups on horseback like this one occur, it is a social as well as a working event. Notice that even the youngest of cowboys enjoy being a part of this.

Branding calves in a corral.

The majority of cattle branding takes place in the spring. This rite of spring has happened here in the Big Timber area for many years. Ranchers, neighbors, and friends all come together and help each other. They visit each other's ranches and help until all the branding is complete. This can take several weeks to accomplish. It is an honor to be invited to help brand someone else's cattle. The work is hard, and it is usually a very long, full day, but the success of the day is celebrated at the end by sharing a meal and stories about the day's events. This is a postcard.

These are the *c.* 1900 registered brands of the Big Timber area. This photograph was taken by Bill Helmer of a painting that was done on a wall at the Grand Hotel.

Lawrence Allestad takes a walk south on McLeod Street with a few of his "friends." Notice the Grand Hotel on the right; on the left is Gust's Department Store, Cole Drug Store, and the bank sign belongs to Citizen's Bank of Big Timber.

Almeda's Café is filled with local cowboys sitting on stools and sharing the news of the day. Today this pastime still remains a cowboy favorite only the location has changed to the Frosty Freeze.

Here is a stunning panoramic view of the mighty Yellowstone River with the majestic Crazy Mountains in the background. With scenery like this, it is no surprise that several movies and a television series have been filmed in the area. The public television station PBS filmed *Frontier House* in the area. It was a reality series about modern-day families living life in the 1800s. Hollywood found the area scenery perfect for filming both *The Horse Whisperer* and *A River Runs Through It.*

The very first Hollywood movie made here was in 1923. It was a Movietone black-and-white silent movie, *A Day With A Forest Ranger.* The moviemakers came to the Main Boulder Ranger Station and made this movie by filming Ranger Harry Kaufman. The movie was made to play before the main feature film, so it is not very long. The complete movie is played for visitors at the restored Main Boulder Ranger Station, shown in this photograph by Leslie Stryker.

122

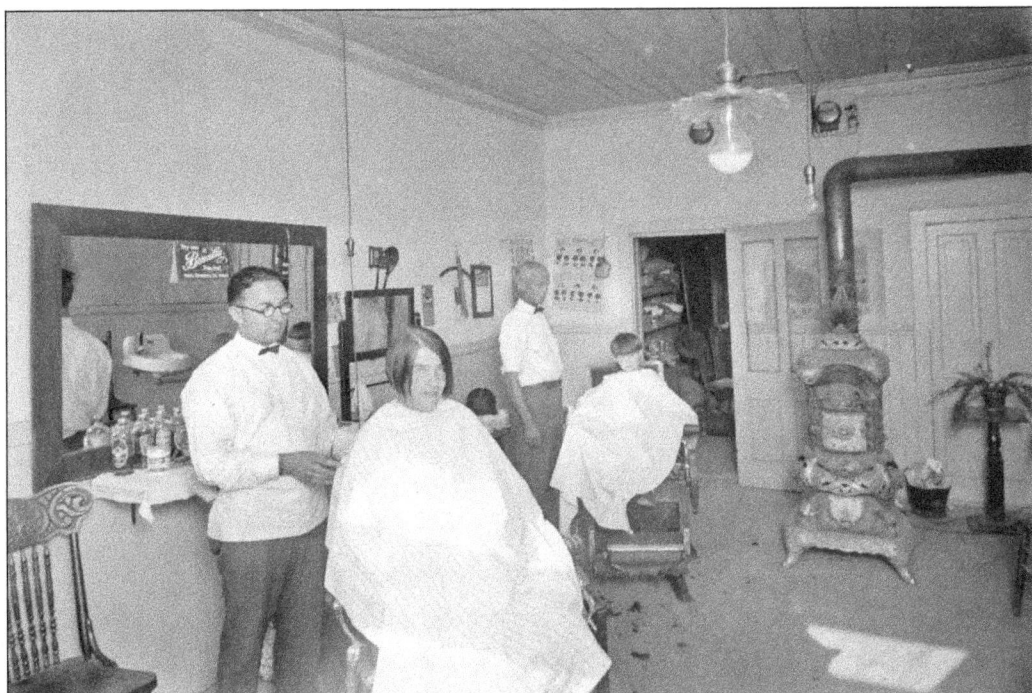

Like any good frontier town, Big Timber continues to have a barbershop. This is an early view of the interior of Jim's Barbershop on McLeod Street.

A parade on McLeod Street with horses and riders draws a lot of spectators. Parades continue to be a favorite of young and old alike. Annual parades take place in the summer for the rodeo, in the fall for high school homecoming, and even in the winter with the annual Lighted Christmas Parade.

BIG TIMBER, MONT

This view of downtown Big Timber looking north on McLeod Street was put on a postcard before 1908.

This block of various businesses is located on the left-hand side of McLeod Street in a view looking south. Notice the building toward the end of the block with the bell tower; at one time, this was the town hall, then it was the fire hall. Today this building is on the National Register of Historic Places.

The east and west sides of McLeod Street are visible in this photograph facing north. Note there are no cars on the street, very unusual. Also the Grand Hotel is on the right side, and the *Big Timber Pioneer* newspaper office is on the left.

This view of McLeod Street faces north toward the Crazy Mountains. Notice that electric streetlight. That streetlight first hung in that intersection in the early 1900s, and it is still hanging in this much later photograph taken by Sanborn.

This is McLeod Street today, facing north toward the Crazy Mountains. That hanging electric light has been replaced by streetlights on the sidewalks up and down the street. (Photograph by Leslie Stryker.)

126

This image shows the Crazy Mountain Museum, located in Big Timber, Montana. The museum is open from May through September. Guided tours are available and there are several out buildings, including a one-room schoolhouse, to tour as well.

Visit us at
arcadiapublishing.com

www.ingramcontent.com/pod-product-compliance
Lightning Source LLC
Chambersburg PA
CBHW080559110426
42813CB00006B/1349